CONSTITUTION

AND

BY-LAWS

OF THE

LINONIAN SOCIETY,

OF YALE COLLEGE.

Instituted 1753.

NEW HAVEN:
PRINTED BY TUTTLE, MOREHOUSE & TAYLOR.
1863.

LINONIA HALL: Wednesday Evening,
April 1st, 1863.

Resolved, That the Committee on Revision be and is hereby instructed to cause to be printed and bound in a convenient form, ten copies of the Constitution and Laws of this Society, one copy of which shall be given to each of the following Officers, viz: the President, Treasurer, Librarian, Secretary and Vice-Secretary, each of whom shall transmit said copy to his successor; and also, that a copy be kept in the President's desk, the remainder to be kept in the Library.

THOMAS A. EMERSON, *President.*

CHARLES M. WHITTELSEY, *Secretary.*

CONSTITUTION

OF THE

LINONIAN SOCIETY.

ARTICLE I.

SECTION I. This Society shall be called LINONIA. Name.

SECTION II. Its object shall be to promote Friendship, Social Intercourse, and Literary Improvement. Object.

ARTICLE II.

SECTION I. Any undergraduate member of the Academic department of Yale College, who has not joined the Society of the Brothers in Unity, may become a member of this Society, by a majority vote of those present at any regular meeting. Membership

Pledge.

SECTION II. Every person when admitted into this Society, must assent to the following pledge :—

YOU PLEDGE YOUR HONOR TO OBEY THE CONSTITUTION AND LAWS OF THE LINONIAN SOCIETY : TO OBSERVE ITS INTERESTS, TO KEEP ITS SECRETS AND TO DO YOUR BEST TO PROMOTE ITS WELFARE. THIS YOU SOLEMNLY PROMISE.

Honorary Members.

SECTION III. Whoever may be recommended by any active member, may be admitted an Honorary member of this Society, on the conditions requisite for regular members.

When active membership ceases.

SECTION IV. Members of the Senior Class shall cease to be *Active*, and shall become *Honorary* members of this Society, on the third regular meeting of the Summer term : but the officers shall continue to serve until the expiration of the terms for which they were elected.

Members leaving College become honorary members.

SECTION V. Any member when no longer in College, shall become an Honorary member of this Society ; but no Honorary member shall vote or hold any office except that of Treasurer or Librarian.

ARTICLE III.

SECTION I. The Officers of this Society shall be a President, and Vice-President from the Senior Class: a Secretary from the Junior Class: a Vice-Secretary from the Sophomore Class: a Treasurer and Librarian, who must be graduate Honorary members of the Society, residing in New Haven: a Prudential Committee, to consist of the President, the Librarian and the Treasurer, and in addition, one member of the Senior and Junior Classes respectively. Officers.

SECTION II. No active member shall be elected twice to the same office, or be eligible to any office unless he be a qualified voter. Qualifications of Officers.

SECTION III. No member shall hold two offices at the same time, except in the cases provided for by the first section in this article. No member can hold two offices.

ARTICLE IV.

SECTION I. It shall be the duty of the PRESIDENT to preside at all meetings of the Society: to give a decision at the close of each debate Duty of the President.

on questions regularly discussed, and to preside at the sessions of the Prudential Committee.

Duties of the Vice-President.

SECTION II. If the President be absent, his duties shall devolve on the VICE-PRESIDENT. If the latter be absent, the Society shall appoint a President *pro tempore.*

Duty of the Secretary.

SECTION III. The SECRETARY shall record the transactions of each meeting, and read them before the Society at each succeeding regular meeting. He shall preserve all written motions, bills and petitions. He shall keep a list of the Active members of the Society, for election and other purposes; and see that every newly elected member signs his name in its appropriate place, in the separate book provided for that purpose: he shall also keep two copies of the Constitution and By-Laws, in which he shall insert all additional clauses and amendments. He shall have one of these copies present at every regular meeting, and shall read from it, just previous to each election, such parts as relate thereto. It shall be the further duty of the

Secretary to cause to be put up in conspicuous places on the morning preceding each regular meeting of the Society, not less than four posters stating the time of meeting, the Literary Appointments of the evening and the subject for Debate.

SECTION IV. The VICE-SECRETARY shall aid the Secretary, when necessary; in the latter's absence perform his duties, and notify appointees of their appointments. Duty of the Vice-Secretary.

SECTION V. The PRUDENTIAL COMMITTEE shall manage the business affairs of the Society, and have a general supervision of the Hall and the Library, subject to such rules as the Society may adopt. They shall make a report at the fourth regular meeting of the Summer term. Duty of the Prudential Committee.

SECTION VI. The TREASURER shall receive from the Treasurer of the College, all monies accruing to the Society from taxes and fines, and shall collect subscriptions, which he shall disburse to the order of the Prudential Committee alone. At the fourth regular meeting of Duty of the Treasurer.

the Summer term, he shall report to the Society his account of receipts and expenditures.

Duty of the Librarian.

SECTION VII. The LIBRARIAN shall have immediate charge of the Library. At the first meeting of the Prudential Committee for each term, he shall present a list of all the books lost or damaged during the preceding term, and record the damages assessed on them by the Committee. He shall inflict all penalties for violating Library Laws, and shall collect, or report to the College Treasurer, all fines and damages; rendering account thereof to the Treasurer of the Society alone. He shall keep the archives of the Society and record all books coming into the Society's possession, and the names of any donors. He shall not permit any person legally excluded from the Library, to draw books either on his own or another's share, nor any person—except in cases which may be provided for—to have access to the Library at any time, other than those specified in the Rules and By-Laws, on pain of forfeiting his office.

ARTICLE V.

SECTION I. The Elections of this Society shall be held on the fourth regular meeting of the Summer term, the fifth and last of the Fall term, the sixth and last of the Spring term. Elections.

SECTION II. At every Election, a President, Vice-President, Secretary and Vice-Secretary shall be chosen: and on the fourth regular meeting of the Summer term, a Treasurer and Prudential Committee. Election of Officers.

SECTION III. The Librarian shall be appointed whenever a vacancy occurs, by the President of the College, on the nomination of the Society, and shall hold office during good behavior. Appointment of Librarian.

SECTION IV. No member shall vote for any officer or appointee, or to impeach any officer, unless he has paid all his fines, damages and taxes. Qualifications of voters.

ARTICLE VI.

SECTION I. The Society shall meet in Lino- Regular meetings.

nia Hall each Wednesday evening of a collegiate term.

Exercises. SECTION II. The regular exercises of each regular meeting, excepting the evening of election, shall be the Secretary's Report, Reading of Questions for Debate, Miscellaneous Business, Composition and Oral Debate: after which the President shall give a decision, both on the merits of the question and the weight of argument, as presented by the disputants.

Orators. SECTION III. At each election meeting, the Society shall elect by ballot a member, either of the Senior or Junior Class, to deliver an Oration at the next election; provided that at the fifth election of the year the members of the Senior class shall elect one of their own number, to deliver a Valedictory Oration on the next election evening.

Readers. SECTION IV. At each regular meeting the President shall appoint a Reader, whose duty it shall be to read before the Society, four weeks after his appointment, a Composition written by himself, and such other Compositions as may be given him for that purpose by any member. The Readers shall be appointed in the order of the classes, beginning with the Senior Class.

SECTION V. On the sixth regular meeting of each term, the President shall appoint three Seniors, two Juniors, two Sophomores and two Freshmen, a committee to choose questions for the ensuing term. They shall announce their choice to the Society, three weeks from the date of their appointment: but the Society has the power to change any question by Substitution, provided it be done two weeks previous to the time for its discussion. Committee on Questions.

SECTION VI. The President or Prudential Committee may call a special meeting at any time: notice of which shall be given by Posters. Special Meetings

ARTICLE VII.

Should this Society ever be dissolved, its Library and other property shall become the property of Yale College.

ARTICLE VIII.

SECTION I. Thirty members shall constitute Quorum.

a quorum for the election of officers, and twenty for Miscellaneous Business.

Impeachment.

SECTION II. Any officer may be impeached for malfeasance in office, if the charges are presented in writing one week beforehand; and a two-thirds vote of the qualified voters present shall remove him from office and expel him from the Society. No person thus removed shall be restored to membership, except by a like vote.

Amendments and additional clauses.

SECTION III. Any proposition to amend or add to the Constitution or By-Laws, if submitted in writing for one week, shall, by a two-thirds vote of the members present, be incorporated in them.

Suspension of Rules

SECTION IV. Any existing rule of the Society may be suspended by a two-thirds vote of the members present: provided however, that the rules for electing officers may in no case be suspended.

Exclusion from the Library.

SECTION V. No member, whose taxes are reported to the Librarian as unpaid, shall be allowed to draw books from the Library.

BY-LAWS

OF THE

LINONIAN SOCIETY.

Article First.

THE LIBRARY.

SECTION I. Books shall be drawn (during term time) under the following Regulations for drawing Books.

RULES.

1. During term time the Library shall be opened for the delivery of books daily, from 1.45 to 2.15 o'clock, P. M., unless the books have been called in by previous notice.

II. All books shall be drawn in the following manner: the drawer shall write on a slip of paper his *name*, and the numbers of the books he wishes, and hand it to one of the Assisting Librarians. The Assisting Librarian shall erase from the list such numbers as are not placed in the drawer's hands, and *check* those which the drawer returns to him. All unchecked numbers shall be considered as retained; and if they be not submitted to the Librarian for charge, the drawer shall be excluded from the Library till they are returned.

III. Encyclopedias may be retained from the Library one week only; all other books three weeks, except when recalled.

IV. No person shall be allowed to call for more than eight books on his own or four on another's share, from which to choose the number that he is entitled to draw.

V. Books must be charged in all cases before they are taken from the Library.

VI. Four volumes only may stand charged to the same name at the same time, and no person may draw books upon the name of any other member, without presenting to the Librarian a request in writing from that member, naming the individual book or books; the said member becoming responsible for any fines assessed upon, or loss of such books.

VII. Books may not be renewed before returning to the shelves.

VIII. During the time of drawing books, no person shall be allowed to pass behind the railing except the Librarian and his Assistants.

IX. Books belonging to the Library shall not be taken out of the City of New Haven.

X. **The acting and graduated members** of the other Societies in College may draw books under the same regulations as acting members of this Society.

XI. **Honorary Members** of this and the other College Societies, may draw books under the same regulations as acting members, by the payment of one dollar a term, in advance, to the Librarian of the Society of which they are members.

PENALTIES.

I. Persons retaining books from the Library for a longer time than above specified, shall be fined one cent per volume for every day of such retention.

II. When the books have been recalled by notice, the above fine shall be increased to ten cents per volume for every day retained.

III. The fine for taking books from the Library uncharged, shall be twenty-five cents per volume.

IV. If books are seriously injured or lost, the person to whom they are charged shall be held responsible to replace them, or pay the cost of replacing them to the Librarian or to the College Treasurer.

V. Persons neglecting or refusing to pay their fines shall not be permitted to draw books until such fines have been paid; and it shall be the duty of the Librarian, in case any person is excluded from the use of this Library, to notify the Librarians of the other Societies, who will also exclude him from the use of their Libraries, until they receive notice from the Librarian of this Society that the cause of exclusion no longer exists.

Section 2. The Library shall be opened for drawing books, the first Saturday of each term, and closed the last Wednesday, unless the Prudential Committee otherwise direct. Opening of the Library.

Section 3. Once in four weeks, the Librarian shall examine his lists; and if he find that any member has retained a book more than one week beyond the lawful time, he shall send him a filled blank, containing the number of the volume, and requiring its immediate return. For each day, after being notified, such member shall be fined ten cents per volume, till it is returned. Any person, moreover, notified to return books, shall be at once excluded from the Library, till the books are brought back, and shall be reported to the Librarian of the Brothers in Unity. Recall of Books.

Section 4. On the last Wednesday of each term, the Librarian shall cause to be posted at least eight notices, in as many conspicuous places, requiring all books to be returned on or before the following Saturday; and no books shall be called in at any other time, unless the Prudential Committee otherwise direct. Notices for returning Books.

Section 5. The Librarian, or some member of the Society whom the Prudential Committee may ap- Drawing of books during vacation.

point, shall, at stated times during the Winter and Spring vacations, allow books to be drawn from the Library, under the regulations contained in the first section of this chapter ; except that no penalties shall be incurred under the operation of the third rule, in case the books thus drawn shall have been returned on or before the last Monday of the vacation. The person thus having charge of the Library shall, on or before the last Wednesday of the vacation, post notices in the manner prescribed in the fourth section of this article, requiring all books belonging to the Library to be returned on or before the following Monday ; and no books shall be drawn from the Library during the Summer vacation.

Assistants.

SECTION 6. The Librarian may appoint two active members of the Society to assist him in delivering books.

Article Second.

FINANCES.

Taxes: when due.

SECTION 1. The regular taxes of each member of this Society shall be two dollars a term : which, together with all fines and damages not otherwise provided for, shall be charged in tha regular term bills, and paid at the office of the College Treasurer.

Subscriptions.

SECTION 2. Subscriptions may be taken up for such purposes, in such a manner and at such times as the Prudential Committee may direct.

SECTION 3. The President shall be exempt from one term's; and the Senior and Junior members of the Prudential Committee from the regular taxes. The members of the Senior class shall be exempt from the regular taxes of their third term. Exempted taxes.

SECTION 4. The Librarian shall receive one hundred and fifty dollars, and the Assistant Librarians shall each receive ten dollars, and be exempt from the taxes of the year.

SECTION 5. So long as any debts remain against the Society, seventy-five per cent. (.75) of the actual income shall be devoted exclusively to the current expenses of the Library and Society Halls, and to the maintenance and increase of the Library, and the remaining twenty-five per cent. (.25) shall form a sinking fund, to liquidate the debt and defray the extraordinary expenses of the Society; such only, as prizes offered by the Society, the publication of Catalogues, the decoration and furnishing of the Halls, and the purchases of works of art. But whenever the Society is free from debt, eighty-five per cent. (.85) shall be devoted to the current expenses and support of Library, as above, and the remaining fifteen per cent. (.15) to the sinking fund. Income.

Article Third.

MEETINGS AND THEIR EXERCISES.

SECTION 1. The order of Exercises at each regular meeting shall be, Order of Exercises.

I. Calling the Society to order at 8 P. M.
II. Reading the report by the Secretary.
III. Miscellaneous Business.
IV. Composition.
V. Appointments.
VI. Reading the questions for the next two weeks, by the President.
VII. Oral Debate.
VIII. The President's Decision.

Order on Election evening.

SECTION 2. On Election evening, the Oration and Composition shall come before the Miscellaneous Business. When this has been finished, the Elections shall be made.

Order.

SECTION 3. Cushing's Manual shall be the parliamentary standard of this Society.

SECTION 4. Any member, rising to speak, shall first address the President; and while a member is speaking, no person shall rise and leave the hall.

Order of Debate.

SECTION 5. The Regular Debate shall be open to any member, who may speak only twice unless by permission of the Society.

Prize Debate.

SECTION 6. No member shall enter any Prize Debate of the Society, who shall not have spoken in the Regular Debates at least twice during each of the two terms immediately preceding the one in which the debate occurs: *provided*, That this rule shall not affect those who may not have entered College in season to comply with it, nor those who may have been prevented from compliance by reason of protracted absence from College duties. It is imperative on the President to see that this regulation is complied with.

SECTION 7. No member shall occupy more than twenty minutes in reading any composition, or shall at any time speak continuously to exceed this limit, unless by unanimous consent.

Article Fourth.

ELECTIONS.

SECTION 1. No officer shall be elected except by ballot. Election by ballot.

SECTION 2. All officers shall be voted for on the same ballot; for which purpose, the Secretary shall provide blanks, with the titles of the offices printed on them. The space between each title shall be filled in with the name of the candidate. All officers voted for on the same ballot.

SECTION 3. The Secretary shall call from the list, kept by himself, the names of the qualified voters, in the order of their classes: the votes of such members shall be deposited in a ballot box guarded by the officiating President. But no vote shall be deposited till the voter's name has been checked by the Secretary, nor shall any voting by proxies be allowed. When the list has been called, the polls shall remain open for three minutes to allow of any corrections. Manner of voting.

SECTION 4. The Secretary, Vice-Secretary and senior member of the Prudential Committee, shall be a committee to sort and count votes. Sorters of Votes.

SECTION 5. All blank votes shall be uncounted: and in every election a majority of votes shall elect. Votes to Elect.

SECTION 6. In case there are more ballots than voters checked, the election shall be void. Election; when void.

Article Fifth.

HALL.

Superintendence

SECTION 1. The Hall of this Society shall be under the general superintendence of the Prudential Committee, who shall see that it and its furnishings are maintained in good condition and repair.

Visitors.

SECTION 2. The Hall shall be accessible to visitors, under such regulations as the Society may establish, but it shall not be used for general College or Class meetings, or for any purposes foreign to the objects of the Society, except by special permission of the Prudential Committee.

Janitor.

SECTION 3. The Prudential Committee may employ a Janitor, at a salary not to exceed fifteen dollars ($15) per term, (inclusive of abatement of taxes, if he is a member of the Society.) He shall have the care of the Hall, and in order that the comfort and interest of the Society may be more certainly secured, certain of his duties are hereby specified.

Janitor's duties.

SECTION 4. He shall sweep the Hall during term time, every week ; he shall see that the Hall is properly warmed, and all its furniture in order and a condition of neatness, at the opening of each regular meeting. He shall see that the windows of the Hall are shut and the doors secured and locked every night, and that the windows are not left open in stormy weather. He shall perform such other duties pertaining to his department as the Prudential Committee may specify.

SECTION 5. For failure or neglect in the performance of the duties above specified, by which the Hall or its furuiture shall incur damage or the members of the Society suffer great inconvenience and discomfort, the Janitor shall forfeit a portion of his salary, at the discretion of the Prudential Committee. Provided however, that the forfeit for any single case of failure or neglect, shall not exceed one third of the term's salary. Penalties.

SECTION 6. One set of keys to the Hall shall be kept by the Janitor, for his exclusive use. One set shall be given to the charge of the Librarian, and one set to the charge of the President. The Librarian and President may loan the keys in their keeping to persons wishing to visit the Hall, but shall not permit the Hall to be opened for any purpose forbidden in the Second Section of this Article, except by authority of the Prudential Committee. Keys.

www.ingramcontent.com/pod-product-compliance
Lightning Source LLC
La Vergne TN
LVHW011146110826
845150LV00008B/2539
* 9 7 8 1 4 1 8 1 9 2 4 2 6 *